The Art of Lesson Planning:
A Practical Guide for Classroom Teachers

By Erica Blatt & Jinyoung Kim
with contributions from Lilian Hopkins

ISOAPPLE®

The Art of Lesson Planning: A Practical Guide for Classroom Teachers
By Erica Blatt & Jinyoung Kim
with contributions from Lilian Hopkins

ISOAPPLE®

2000 Bigler St. #A
Fort Lee, NJ 07024
201/676-0247
201/944-2310

Find us on the World Wide Web at : www.isoapple.com
To report errors, Please send a note to publishing@isoapple.com
Copyright © 2011 by ISOAPPLE
Cover Illustration and Book Designed by ISOAPPLE

Notice of Rights
All rights reserved. No part of this book may be reproduced or transmitted in any form by any means, electronic, mechanical, photocopying, recording, or otherwise, without the prior written permission of the publisher. For information on getting permission for reprints and excerpts, contact publishing@isoapple.com

Notice of Liability
The information in this book is distributed on an "As Is" basis, without warranty. While every precaution has been taken in the preparation of the book, neither the author nor ISOAPPLE shall have any liability to any person or entity with respect to any loss or damage caused or alleged to be caused directly or indirectly by the instructions contained in this book.

ISBN 978-0-9850012-0-9

Printed and bound in the United States of America

TABLE OF CONTENTS

Introduction — 1

Lesson Plan Contents — 5

    Lesson Information — 6

    Prerequisite Knowledge — 7

    Vocabulary and Definitions — 9

    Standards — 11

    Objectives — 16

    Materials — 21

    Procedure — 22

        Introduction — 24

        Motivation — 26

        Mini-Lesson — 28

        Group Work — 34

        Share — 38

        Conclusion — 40

    Time Allotment — 41

    Formative Assessment — 42

    Handouts — 46

    Extension/Follow-up Activity — 47

References — 49

Glossary of Terms — 51

Appendix A : Lesson Plan Comments — 55

Appendix B : Example of Science Lesson Plan — 65

Appendix C : Example of Music Lesson Plan — 75

PREFACE

This booklet is written for pre-service teachers in an education program, who are in the process of learning how to write a lesson plan. This booklet is an introduction to the basic format of a lesson plan, and includes a specific structure for writing a lesson plan. We have included examples in each section, as well as exercises to help pre-service teachers gain a better understanding of what to include and not include in each section.

As university professors of a multi-disciplinary teaching methods course (Teaching Math, Science, and Music in Elementary Education), we decided to write this book because in our experiences working with pre-service teachers, we found that providing students with a written explanation of the various parts of a lesson is necessary for students developing an understanding of how to thoroughly write their own lesson plans. It is our hope that the detailed description of each section of a lesson plan will clarify for pre-service teachers what is appropriate in each section, and provide them with an easy-to-follow format that can be applied to multiple subjects. The examples provided in this booklet are based on topics in the standards for the lower grades in the subjects of math, science, and music, as these are the specialty areas of the authors.

The contents of this booklet are based on our interactions with our students and observations of our students' written lesson plans. In response to our notations and analysis of frequent student errors, we have tried to address commonly made mistakes and point out ways to appropriately conceptualize the parts of the lesson and how they fit together. As we continue to work with pre-service teachers and teach the art of lesson planning, we will develop this booklet further to elaborate on the contents where necessary. Hopefully, you will find this booklet to be useful in your planning and teaching lessons now and in the future.

We would like to acknowledge our colleague Gail Rosenberg, as well as our other colleagues, in the Department of Education at the College of Staten Island, CUNY, for their input and feedback in developing this booklet.

Erica Blatt and Jinyoung Kim
Department of Education, College of Staten Island, CUNY

August 2011

INTRODUCTION

*A lesson plan is like a map that will guide you through your teaching experience.
In creating this map, or lesson plan, you need to think through the journey on which you want
to lead your students in order to reach a specific destination.*

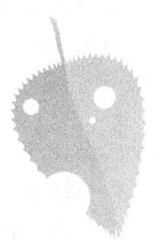

WHY IS A LESSON PLAN IMPORTANT?

A lesson plan is like a map that will guide you through your teaching experience. In creating this map, or lesson plan, you need to think through the journey on which you want to lead your students in order to reach a specific destination. Planning for your teaching in advance allows you to prepare a lesson that meets its objectives by keeping students engaged through multiple activities.

A lesson plan, like a map, can be written in many different formats at differing levels of detail. The structure of the lesson plan we are using in this booklet is commonly used among pre-service teacher educators because it provides a format that allows for in depth contents in each of the sections of the lesson plan. The key parts of this lesson plan format include the introduction, motivation, mini-lesson, group work, share, and conclusion. Each of these sections is explained in detail along with examples and exercises in the text of this booklet. In each section, there are other terms commonly used for that section of the lesson plan. For example, the group work section of the lesson plan may also be called "coached practice" in other contexts. If you are using a different lesson plan format in your future teaching, the contents of each section are transferrable.

In addition, a lesson plan has other elements that are necessary to align the lesson plan with the curriculum and national, state, or local standards. These elements include the grade level, topic, lesson objectives, and standards, which are important parts of the system of accountability in the field of education. This system of accountability has been developed to ensure that teachers in different localities are teaching the same core set of concepts to students at the different grade levels. Each subject area has its own set of standards that have been created by professional organizations at the national and state level, providing guidance for teachers regarding the scope and sequence of the topics to be taught. The standards for the areas of science, math, and music are discussed further in the pages to follow.

A final section of each lesson plan should provide an outline of assessment strategies utilized in the lesson. This is critical for teachers in planning how they will measure if the lesson's objectives are achieved during the lesson. A discussion about the various forms of formal and informal assessment is included in the section about assessment strategies.

In other coursework and your future teaching setting, you may not be required to write your lesson plans in as much depth as is recommended in this booklet. So, why should you do it now? This is a question that we have been asked often by our students. The answer is three-fold:

- First, as a pre-service teacher, it is necessary to prepare as thoroughly as possible, which will raise your confidence as you step into the classroom.

- Second, by writing in each section specific activities, instructions, and questions and answers, this provides pre-service teachers with the opportunity to both think about and express what is going to occur during the lesson.

- Third, in addition to the benefits for you as a pre-service teacher, your lesson plan is an indication to your professor (or principal, in the future) that you are fully prepared to work with students.

Another important feature of this particular lesson plan format is that it includes activities that incorporate the different learning styles of different types of learners. For example, it is recommended that you use visual aids (such as a dry erase board) during the motivation and mini-lesson sections of your lesson plan to enhance learning for visual learners. It is also important to include questioning throughout the lesson to assist auditory learners who learn best through hearing explanations from both the instructor and their peers. The process of questioning also develops students' reasoning skills, as they are required to think about the concepts and apply them in new ways. Additionally, for kinesthetic (or hands-on) learners, it is critical to include a hands-on part of the lesson, in which students are using manipulative materials to construct their own knowledge about the topic of the lesson. Finally, this lesson format includes a group work section, which allows students the opportunity to learn to work with their peers and develop essential communication skills.

The content of this booklet is organized according to the order that it should be written in the recommended lesson plan format. This should also be congruent with your thinking cycle as you go through the process of creating a lesson plan, beginning with the objectives, leading to the lesson procedure, and followed by your assessment strategies, which should ensure that you are meeting your lesson objectives.

As you read through this booklet, you will find in each section an explanation of the lesson plan section and definitions of key words, what to include and not include in the section, why the section of the lesson plan is necessary, examples from each subject (math, music, and science), and exercises that provide practice with what to include in the section. As some of the examples may be topics that you will use in your own lessons, it is expected that you will modify these examples and add your own ideas to make the lesson appropriate for the context in which you are teaching. You will find at the end of the booklet a glossary of key terms, as well as references cited throughout the booklet. Finally, the appendix includes a list of common errors that you should refer to in revising your own lesson plans.

INTRODUCTION

The lesson plan format that you will be introduced to in this booklet will lead you to confident and enjoyable teaching that you will be able to utilize in the years ahead. It is important to remember that even though lesson planning has a specific structure, it is your unique ideas and activities that will make the lesson engaging for your students. To return to our analogy, lesson planning is drawing the map that will guide you in your teaching; however, you must take the steps necessary to lead your students down this path in order to make your lesson plan a reality.

LESSON PLAN CONTENTS

The lesson plan format that you will be introduced to in this booklet will lead you to confident and enjoyable teaching that you will be able to utilize in the years ahead.

Lesson Information
(Includes Subject, Topic, Number, Teaching Date, Grade Level)

Each lesson plan should include which subject is being taught and the general topic of the lesson. You should also indicate the number of the lesson within a unit or within the curriculum and the date the lesson will be taught, which provides information regarding the sequence of the curriculum and pre-requisite knowledge you should consider in planning your lesson. Additionally, the grade level of the target audience should be included in order to indicate developmentally appropriate practices to be utilized in the lesson, in addition to the standards that should be addressed.

Example 1

Subject: Math
Topic: **Telling Time on an Analog Clock Lesson**
Number: 1
Teaching Date: October 12, 2011
Grade Level: 2nd Grade

Example 2

Subject: Science
Topic: **Comparing Temperatures**
Lesson Number: 2
Teaching Date: April 9, 2012
Grade Level: 1st Grade CTT

Example 3

Subject: Music
Topic: **Beat and Rhythm**
Lesson Number: 2
Teaching Date: November 24, 2012
Grade Level: 2nd Grade

Prerequisite Knowledge

Prerequisite knowledge is what is required for students to know in order to participate successfully in the lesson. This includes key ideas which have been learned in a previous lesson or years of schooling, or through personal experience. In the case of previous years of schooling, these ideas are often located within the standards documents for the subject being taught. It is important to include a description of the prerequisite knowledge because this is the scaffolding that students should have prior to encountering this lesson. The teacher should begin each lesson by assessing students' prerequisite knowledge in order to determine the level of students' understanding, and whether a review of this knowledge is required before continuing with new information.

Prerequisite knowledge should not include a listing of contents to be taught in the given lesson, unrelated topics, or specific experiences outside of school. For example, in order to learn about different types of sand, a student does not have to have had previous experiences at the beach (although you may ask students about this type of experience to help them make personal connections with the topic).

Example 1 — Math, Telling Time on Analog Clocks, 2nd Grade

Prerequisite Knowledge:
Students should be able to skip count by fives.

Example 2 — Science, Comparing Temperature, 1st Grade CTT

Prerequisite Knowledge:
Students should be familiar with concepts related to hot and cold.

Example 3 — Music, Beat and Rhythm, 2nd Grade

Prerequisite Knowledge:
Students should be able to differentiate steady and non-steady sound.

LESSON PLAN CONTENTS

✓ Exercise A

Place a checkmark next to the statements that would be appropriate for the above lessons and explain why each would or would not be appropriate.

π Math

___1. Students should be able to tell time to the nearest hour.
___2. Students should understand the function of the long and short hand of the clock.
___3. Students should be able to tell time on a digital clock.

🧪 Science

___1. Students should have experience using a thermometer.
___2. Students should understand that temperature changes in different locations.
___3. Students should know the difference between inside and outside.

♪ Music

___1. Students should have basic knowledge of fractions, such as ½, ¼.
___2. Students should be able to differentiate between long and short sounds.
___3. Students should have basic knowledge of the sounds different musical instruments make.

Vocabulary and Definitions

The **vocabulary** includes the key terms you are teaching in the lesson, and the definitions are the meanings of the key terms. Definitions written on lesson plans include dictionary definitions and kid-friendly definitions, which are more appropriate for the lower grades. When writing kid-friendly definitions, be sure that your definition is both easy to understand and <u>maintains the meaning of the term</u>. It is important for the teacher to fully understand the vocabulary and definitions in order to both translate the meaning to kid-friendly language and to teach the concepts accurately. The appropriate choice of vocabulary for a lesson should be related to the content suggested by the standards for that grade level. For example, it is appropriate for the vocabulary for a second grade lesson on plant parts to include "root," "stem," "leaf," and "flower" but it is inappropriate to include the term "photosynthesis" as this term is not taught until later elementary grades.

In order to determine the best definition to use for your lesson, you should consult several dictionary sources, and find a definition that best fits the focus of the lesson and is written in non-technical language that you can understand. You should then think about the way you will teach this term to the students, and create the kid-friendly definition based on your understanding.

It is important to understand that the purpose of teaching vocabulary is not for students to memorize definitions, but rather to understand the application within the context of the lesson and to begin to be able to utilize the term when appropriate in other settings.

Example 1   Math, Telling Time on Analog Clocks, 2nd Grade

Vocabulary

1. Analog clock: A clock that displays the time of day by the position of the hands on a clock

   Kid-friendly *A clock that has moving hands and the hours are marked from 1 to 12*

Example 2   Science, Comparing Temperature, 1st Grade CTT

Vocabulary

1. Temperature: the degree or intensity of heat present in a substance or object

   Kid-friendly *the amount of heat in an object*

Example 3   Music, Beat and Rhythm, 2nd Grade

Vocabulary

1. Rhythm: the pattern of musical movement through time

   Kid-friendly *the pattern of long and short sounds*

☑ Exercise B

Find the following terms in the dictionary and then translate each term into kid-friendly language.

♪ Music

Beat

Dictionary: _____

Kid-friendly: _____

🧪 Science

Heat

Dictionary: _____

Kid-friendly: _____

π Math

Digital Clock

Dictionary: _____

Kid-friendly: _____

Standards

In the context of education, *standards* are elements which specify the knowledge or skills that students must acquire within a curriculum framework. Standards have been created to provide a guide for teachers in establishing expectations for what students ought to achieve at the various grade levels. Within a teaching unit, standards specify the scope of the content and skills to be taught; however, it is the role of the teacher to divide this content and skills into individual lessons.

The standards for each subject area have been developed by various organizations at the local, state, and national levels:

Science Standards
National, State, and NYC

The *National Science Education Standards* were developed in 1996 by the National Research Council (*www.nap.edu/html/nses/*), whose members are drawn from the councils of the National Academy of Sciences, the National Academy of Engineering, and the Institute of Medicine, to provide a direction for successful science education reform in the effort to produce scientifically literate students. It provides science standards for teaching, professional development, assessment, science content, and science programs. This document provides the science teaching profession with guidelines to be used for planning, organizing, developing, implementing, and evaluating science curricula and programs, and serves as the basis for most state standards documents.

The *New York State Learning Standards and Core Curriculum* is a series of documents developed by the New York State Education Department establishing guidelines for what should be learned by students in Grades K-4, 5-8, and in high school (9-12) in the subjects of the Living Environment, Earth Science, Chemistry, and Physics (*http://www.p12.nysed.gov/ciai/cores.html*) This set of standards does not provide a curriculum framework for each grade level, but rather a list of inquiry and process skills, as well as content standards to be learned within the listed set of grades. The *New York State Learning Standards and Core Curriculum* documents are the foundation upon which State assessments are developed and aligned, and the accountability status for each local school and district is based on State assessment scores. These guidelines serve as the basis for local curriculum frameworks within the state of New York, such as the NYC K-8 Science Scope and Sequence.

The *NYC K-8 Science Scope and Sequence* has been developed by the NYC Department of Education to provide specific standards of what students should know and be able to do at the various grade levels as a result of skilled science instruction. This document lists general process and inquiry skills that students should acquire, as well as detailed units of content to be taught in each grade. For example, the units in Grade 1 include Animal Diversity, Properties of Matter, and Weather and Seasons. The units are broken down into specific standards that can be used as the topics for individual lessons. This is the document that elementary and middle school teachers in the New York City public schools must incorporate into their science instruction. On the first page of the **Scope and Sequence** document is a list of inquiry skills, while the second page contains a list of process skills. Each of your lessons should include at least one inquiry and one process skill which should be listed with the content standard(s) on your lesson plan. Each type of standard should be labeled, as in the example below. Most lessons should cover only one content standard, but in the case of overlap of topics between standards, more than one may be listed.

High school teachers in New York City utilize the Core Curriculum for the NY State Education Department Regents courses of the Living Environment, Earth Science, Chemistry, and Physics, as well as a NYC Department of Education document entitled the NYC High School Science Regents Scope & Sequence, which provides a sequence of units and topics to be followed during the Regents courses.

Elementary: NYC K-8 Science Scope and Sequence
http://schools.nyc.gov/Documents/STEM/Science/K8ScienceSS.pdf

High School: New York State Science Core Curricula for Regents Courses
http://schools.nyc.gov/Academics/Science/EducatorResources/New+York+State+Science+Core+Curricula.htm

NYC High School Science Regents Scope & Sequence
http://schools.nyc.gov/Documents/STEM/Science/HSScienceSSRegents.pdf

---

Example — Science, Comparing Temperature, 1st Grade CTT

Content Standard:
PS 1.1a, PS 3.1g Compare temperatures in different locations (e.g., inside, outside, in the sun, in the shade).

Inquiry Skills Standards:
Gathering and organizing data – collecting information about objects and events which illustrate a specific situation
Manipulating materials – handling or treating materials and equipment safely, skillfully, and effectively

Process Skills Standards:
iv. Manipulate materials through teacher direction and free discovery.
xx. Compare and contrast organisms/objects/events in the living and physical environments.

Math Standards
National, State, and NYC

In 2000, the National Council of Teachers of Mathematics released the **Principles and Standards for School Mathematics (PSSM)**, which were created using a consensus process involving mathematicians, teachers, and educational researchers. More recently, a state-led effort has produced **The Common Core State Standards**, which has been sponsored by the National Governors Association Center for Best Practices (NGA Center) and the Council of Chief State School Officers (CCSSO). The standards were developed in collaboration with teachers, school administrators, and experts, to provide a framework for establishing a common understanding of what students are expected to learn. These standards define the knowledge and skills students should have within their K-12 education, so that they graduate high school able to succeed in academic college courses and in workforce training programs. These standards endeavor to present a sequence of topics and performances that are logical and reflect the sequential and hierarchical nature of mathematics. Moreover, the standards stress not only the conceptual understaing of key ideas, but also continually return to the organizing principles of mathematics such as place value or the laws of arithmetic to structure those ideas (*http://www.corestandards.org*). **The Common Core Standards** were released for mathematics in June, 2010, with a majority of states adopting the standards in the subsequent months, which will likely impact the New York State standards in coming years.

New York City currently uses the **New York State Mathematics Core Curriculum** standards for math, which were revised in 2005. There are 10 standards for each grade level: 5 process standards and 5 content standards. The process standards are: problem solving, reasoning and proof, communication, connections, and representation. The five content standards are: number sense and operations, algebra, geometry, measurement, and statistics and probability.

New York State Core Curriculum (revised 2005)
www.p12.nysed.gov/ciai/mst/math/standards/core.html

Example — Math, Telling Time on Analog Clocks, 2nd grade

Content Standard:
2.M.9 Tell time to the half hour and five minutes using an analog clock.

Process Skills Standards:
2.PS.9 Use drawings/pictures to model the action in problems.

Music Standards
National and State

For music standards, you can refer to the standards developed by the New York State School Music Association (NYSSMA) and/or the ones by the National Association for Music Education (MENC).

NYSSMA has developed the 4 general learning standards for the arts to reflect educational goals that are common to dance, music, theatre, and the visual arts:

- Standard 1: Creating, Performing and Participating in the Arts
  Students will actively engage in the processes that constitute creation and performance in the arts(dance, music, theatre, and visual arts) and participate in various roles in the arts.

- Standard 2: Knowing and Using Arts Materials and Resources
  Students will be knowledgeable about and make use of the materials and resources available for participation in the arts in various roles.

- Standard 3: Responding to and Analyzing Works of Art
  Students will respond critically to a variety of works in the arts, connecting the individual work to other works and to other aspects of human endeavor and thought.

- Standard 4: Understanding the Cultural Dimensions and Contributions of the Arts
  Students will develop an understanding of the personal and cultural forces that shape artistic communication and how the arts in turn shape the diverse cultures of past and present society.

 Learning Standards for Arts incorporate the content standards and performance indicators according to each discipline and different learning level.
(See more detailed standards at *http://www.p12.nysed.gov/ciai/arts/pub/artlearn.pdf*).

National music standards include the following 9 content standards:
1. Singing, alone and with others, a varied repertoire of music.
2. Performing on instruments, alone and with others, a varied repertoire of music.
3. Improvising melodies, variations, and accompaniments.
4. Composing and arranging music within specified guidelines.
5. Reading and notating music.
6. Listening to, analyzing, and describing music.
7. Evaluating music and music performances.
8. Understanding relationships between music, the other arts, and disciplines outside the arts.
9. Understanding music in relation to history and culture.

These content standards are further articulated into achievement standards according to children's age/grade level (see *http://www.menc.org/resources/view/the-school-music-program-a-new-vision* for more detail of **The National Association for Music Education K-4 Standards**)

> **Example** Music, Beat and Rhythm, 2nd Grade
>
> **Content Standard:**
> Reading and notating music
>
> **Achievement Standard:**
> Students
> a. read whole, half, dotted half, quarter, and eighth notes and rests in 24, 34, and 44 meter signatures
> b. use standard symbols to notate meter, rhythm, pitch, and dynamics in simple patterns presented by the teacher

Objectives (Cognitive, Affective, and Psychomotor)

The **objectives**, i.e. instructional objectives (or educational goals), are the teacher's specific goals for what the students will accomplish during the lesson. These objectives should specify the learning outcomes that you want students to achieve and should be measurable. There are three types of objectives, including cognitive, affective, and psychomotor, which are associated with the developmental domains originated from Bloom's taxonomy (reference three handbooks from Bloom).

Cognitive objectives describe the goals for students' acquisition of knowledge and critical thinking skills. This goes beyond students' comprehension of terms, and includes analysis and application of the concepts.

Affective objectives are related to students' feelings, attitudes, and emotions. During an educational experience, these objectives encompass students' expression of thoughts or feelings, and ability to work effectively with others.

Psychomotor (or behavioral) objectives involve the development of physical skills and often involve manipulation of materials. It is important for each lesson to include objectives in all three domains in order to encourage the holistic development of students' minds, feelings, and motor skills.

To write an objective, you should begin with a statement describing what the target audience will be able to do by the end of the lesson. For example, "By the end of the lesson, students will be able to…." or "By completing this lesson, students will…" After this statement, you should utilize a verb appropriate for the given domain, followed by a specific, concise outcome that you want students to accomplish. It is important to remember that your objectives should be more specific than what is listed in the standards because the standards are written for general usage, and your objectives need to provide a narrower focus for the lesson. Moreover, you should not simply list what you will do as an activity because an objective is not what students will do, but rather what students will achieve through what they do. For example, if students are writing as part of the lesson, your objective should be about what the students will accomplish through writing, such as "the students will be able to differentiate between (two concepts) in their writing" (cognitive), "the students will be able to express their opinion through writing" (affective), "the students will be able to practice their hand-eye coordination through writing" (psychomotor).

Cognitive Objectives

It is important that your cognitive objectives include the specific elements that you want students to learn. For example, when writing the cognitive objective in Example 2 below on comparing temperature, it would not be specific enough to write "Students will be able to compare temperatures in different locations." Rather, the specific locations need to be written as part of your objective.

Appropriate Verbs: identify, compare/contrast, differentiate, describe, classify, explain, summarize, predict, distinguish, sequence, interpret, solve, calculate

Example 1   Math, Telling Time on Analog Clocks, 2nd grade

By the end of the lesson, students will be able to:

Correctly read various times on an analog clock to five minute intervals.

Example 2   Science, Comparing Temperature, 1st Grade CTT

By the end of the lesson, students will be able to:

Compare temperatures in different locations, including inside and outside the classroom, in the sun, and in the shade.

Example 3   Music, Beat and Rhythm, 2nd Grade

Upon completion of the lesson, students will….

Identify the name and values of musical symbols, such as whole note, half note, quarter note, and eighth note.

Affective Objectives

It is important when writing your affective objectives to consider the meaning of the verb in your objective in a content-specific manner. For example, when you use the word "share" in a science context, this will likely mean sharing the results of an activity or experiment with others, which leads to enhanced communication. However, in the context of a music lesson, sharing a musical piece would likely involve psychomotor skills, such as playing an instrument or singing, which would therefore not be considered an affective objective.

Appropriate Verbs: cooperate, work collaboratively with, share, express, communicate, paying attention, negotiate, respect, appreciate (ex. other's work)

Example

During the lesson, students will:
- Work collaboratively with their partner during group work
- Be paying attention to other students' presentations
- Be able to express their feelings through artwork (or writing)

Psychomotor Objectives

Appropriate Verbs: compose, create, perform, play, record, write, draw, sing, clap, collect, construct, illustrate, arrange, experiment (test), observe

Example 1 — Math, Telling Time on Analog Clocks, 2nd grade

By the end of the lesson, students will be able to:
- Correctly fill in the parts of an analog clock.
- Indicate on a clock a given time to a five minute interval.

Example 2 — Science, Comparing Temperature, 1st Grade CTT

By the end of the lesson, students will be able to:
- Measure temperatures with thermometer in different locations, including inside and outside the classroom, in the sun, and in the shade.
- Record the temperature in degrees Fahrenheit in an organizational chart

Example 3 — Music, Beat and Rhythm, 2nd Grade

Upon completion of the lesson, students will….
- Create a rhythmic pattern of 3 or 4 beats using different musical notes
- Sing rhythmic pattern arranged by different musical notes accurately

LESSON PLAN CONTENTS

✓ Exercise C

C-1: Choose the best **cognitive objective** for the following topic and explain why the other options are not appropriate.

> **Learning about Plant Parts, 2nd Grade**
>
> Students will be able to:
> 1. Identify all of the plant parts.
> 2. Identify several plant parts, including roots, stem, leaves, and flower.
> 3. Communicate with others about the parts of a plant, including roots, stem, leaves, and flower.
> 4. Draw and label all of the plant parts, including roots, stem, leaves, and flower.

C-2: Choose the best **affective objective** for the following topic and explain why the other options are not appropriate.

> **Learning about Musical Instruments, 3rd Grade**
>
> Students will be able to:
> 1. Play musical instruments with their peers.
> 2. Learn how various instruments make sound with their peers.
> 3. Express their mood of the day through playing an instrument.
> 4. Express their opinion of their favorite musical group.

C-3: Choose the best **psychomotor objective** for the following topic and explain why the other options are not appropriate.

> **Learning about Shapes, 1st Grade**
>
> Students will be able to:
> 1. Identify the name of different shapes, including triangle, rectangle, circle, and square.
> 2. Place several smaller shapes together to make a larger shape.
> 3. Work collaboratively to place several smaller shapes together to make a larger shape.
> 4. Categorize objects by their shapes.

Materials

Materials are physical objects that are needed to successfully carry out your lesson plan. Materials include all of the following: visual aids, books, CDs, CD player, worksheets, handouts, Smart Board, dry erase board, computer, musical instruments, art supplies, writing materials, and all manipulatives for hands-on activities. In describing the materials for your lesson, make sure to include how many students for which you are planning the lesson, as well as how many of each item are needed for that group size. When using a specific book, poem, or CD for your lesson, make sure to include the author/composer and title. If you are using materials from a website to aid in the creation of your lesson, you should include a link to the original website within your lesson plan. It is encouraged that you adapt or modify these materials to the specific context of your lesson, rather than copying and pasting the exact format.

It is important for you to include a full list of materials for the lesson for several reasons:

- First, it is useful in your planning to think through the exact number of each material ahead of time, so that you can be fully prepared for your lesson.

- Second, it is informative for a reader of your lesson plan to anticipate what types of materials will be used for the activities in your lesson.

- Third, it is common for teachers to share lesson plans with their colleagues, and it is therefore important to accurately state the number of students and amount of each item, so that others may know the quantity of supplies that they would need for their own group of students.

Example

Materials (8 students, 4 groups)
- 8 Vocabulary Handouts
- 1 Book – "Are you my mother?" By P.D. Eastman
- 8 Pencils
- 1 Dry Erase Board
- 2 Dry Erase Markers
- 20 Animal Picture Cards
- 8 Scissors
- 4 Sets of Animal Cut-Outs (1 per group)
- 4 Pieces of Construction Paper (1 per group)
- 4 Boxes of Crayons (1 per group)
- 4 Glue Sticks
- 8 worksheets for extension (follow-up) activity

Procedure of the Lesson Plan

The procedure of the lesson plan includes the sequence of activities in your lesson, divided into the following sections: introduction, motivation, mini-lesson, group work/coached practice, share, conclusion. While this is a common sequence for the sections of the lesson, it is possible to combine sections or reverse the order of certain sections. For example, it is often beneficial in a science lesson to have students complete their group work or inquiry experience before the mini-lesson, so that students can experiment in a hands-on manner with the material in order to construct their own understanding before being given a full explanation by the teacher.

Within each section of the lesson plan, you need to include a list of the activities and the key questions and answers that you will use during that part of the lesson. The activities in your lesson include all the intended actions that either you or the students will perform. Your list of the major activities should be numbered and clearly state the person doing the action (ex. I (teacher) or students). Sub-activities should be prefaced by Capital Letters (A, B, C) in order to maintain consistency.

The key questions in each section are a vital component of your lesson because they are intended to promote students' thinking about the topic. It is critical that your questions challenge students to go beyond surface-level definitions, and encourage them to develop skills related to application and analysis of the lesson topic. Therefore, your questions should be open-ended whenever possible, and you should limit the number of "yes/no" questions that you are asking. While writing your key questions, it is important to anticipate how you will respond to students' answers which are incorrect. Be ready with follow-up questions to try to figure out why a student is unsure or providing an incorrect answer, rather than just asking another student for the correct answer. This is one of the most important forms of assessment that you will use in teaching!

Along with each question, you need to provide an answer in parentheses. During the introduction, you should include expected student answers and label them as such, ex. "(expected answer: …..)." With an open-ended question in the introduction, you should list a few expected answers, and may then write "answers will vary." In the other sections of your lesson plan, it is important to convey your understanding of the correct answer. If a question has only one correct answer, then this answer should be written in parentheses. If a question is open-ended and has several possible answers, then you should list a few correct answers, and may then write "answers will vary." Knowing the correct answer is essential to be able to convey the proper information to your students. When asking students to define the vocabulary for the lesson, it is appropriate to write the kid-friendly definition as the answer to the question. Key questions should be indented and bulleted under the relevant activity or sub-activity.

> **Example** — Example of Activity/Question Structure
>
> ### Introduction
> 1. I will begin the lesson by asking students the following questions:
>   - o   [Write Key Question Here] (Expected Answer:____)
>   - o   [Write Key Question Here] (Expected Answer:____)
>
> ### Motivation
> 1. I will [add action verb here to indicate activity].
> 2. I will follow up with the following questions:
>   - o   [Write Key Question Here] (Expected Answer:____)
>   - o   [Write Key Question Here] (Expected Answer:____)
>
> ### Mini-Lesson
> 1. I will introduce the new vocabulary terms to the students.
>
> A. We will discuss the definition for [Insert Term Here].
>   - o   Can anyone define the term [Insert Term Here]? ([Insert Correct Kid-friendly Definition Here])
>
> B. We will discuss the definition for [Insert Term Here].
>   - o   Can anyone define the term [Insert Term Here]? ([Insert Correct Kid-friendly Definition Here])
>
> **Lesson Plan continues from here.**

Introduction

The *introduction* is the part of the lesson during which you introduce the topic of your lesson to the students. An effective strategy for the introduction is to ask the students questions related to the lesson topic in order to assess their prior knowledge and to help them make connections with the topic from their previous experiences. The suggested time for the introduction is 3-5 minutes, which is enough time for a series of questions. In the introduction, you are assessing students' understanding of the topic, rather than correcting their answers. In writing the answers to the key questions in your lesson plan, it is therefore appropriate to write the expected student answers to these questions. In your first question, you may use this time to learn students' names and ask them questions about themselves and their experiences, but remember that these should still be related to the topic of the lesson. For example, when teaching students a lesson on animals, it is appropriate to ask them about their favorite animal, but not to ask them about their favorite flavor of ice cream.

> **For Your Information**
>
> In some schools, it is common to have a "Do Now" activity written on the board when students begin a lesson. This is usually independent work that is meant to engage students in the topic right upon entering the classroom. This may take the place of an introduction, as it serves as an educational strategy to gain students' focus at the beginning of the lesson.

> **Example** Science, Rocks, 2nd Grade
>
> **Introduction** (3 minutes)
>
> 1. I will begin the lesson by asking students the following questions:
>
>   - Can anyone tell me about where you might find different rocks?
>   (Expected Answer: in the mountains, playground, park, answers may vary)
>
>   - Can you describe a rock that you have seen?
>   (Expected Answer: hard, gray/black, bumpy, big/small, heavy, answers may vary)

☑ Exercise D

List some possible questions for the introduction of a lesson on the following topics:

♪ Music

1. Musical Instruments

■ _____ ?

■ _____ ?

π Math

2. Clocks

■ _____ ?

■ _____ ?

🧪 Science

3. Plant Part Functions

■ _____ ?

■ _____ ?

Motivation

The **motivation** section of your lesson plan is an activity designed to get students engaged in the lesson. It is important because when students are interested or excited about a topic, then they are more likely to pay attention and engage in active learning. An effective way to motivate students is through creating an activity that utilizes several of the senses, such as visual, auditory, and kinesthetic. This activity should be clearly related to the lesson topic, and not focused only on entertaining the students. Appropriate activities might include: reading a book or poem, listening to or singing a song, playing a simple game, doing a demonstration, watching a video clip, drawing or writing about a related experience, etc. The time frame for the motivation section should be 5-7 minutes.

Example — Music, Teaching About Tempo, 2nd Grade

Motivation (5 minutes)

1. I will play "Flight of the Bumblebee" by Nikolai Rimsky-Korsakov on the CD player.

2. Students will listen to the music and share their feelings related to the music.

    o   What feelings does this music create for you?
        (Expected Answer: busy, anxious, excited, answers will vary)

    o   Why do you think this music gives you these feelings?
        (Expected Answer: because it is fast)

    o   Can anyone tell me the term for fastness or slowness of the music?
        (Expected Answer: tempo)

Exercise E

Think about and write three creative activities for each topic that could be used for the motivation section of a lesson plan on the following concepts.

Math — Different values of change (penny, nickel, dime, quarter)

Music — Different pitches (high or low sounds)

Science — Float or Sink

Mini-Lesson

The **mini-lesson** (or lesson development) section of the lesson plan is where you will teach the vocabulary terms and the key concepts of your lesson. This is the part of the lesson where the core ideas will be conveyed to the students. In order to teach the vocabulary and concepts, it is useful to utilize a visual aid, such as a dry erase board, poster, flash cards, or picture representation. While part of the mini-lesson involves defining the terms with the students, your activities and questions should also help the students to understand the context and application of the terms.

There are several different approaches you can take when designing your mini-lesson. One approach is to introduce the students to the new vocabulary first, and then proceed with an activity that reinforces the students' understanding of these terms and their applications (see Science example below). Another approach is to teach the terms while involving the students in an activity. For example, in a music lesson, to teach the term "beat" you may want to have students tap the steady beat, ask them to describe the sound they just made, and then teach them the actual vocabulary term "beat" (see Music example in Appendix C). A third approach to the mini-lesson is to introduce the students to one vocabulary term, and then do a short activity to demonstrate the meaning. This would be followed by introduction to a second term with a demonstration activity. This approach is useful when it is important for students to understand the first term fully because it is required for the understanding of the second term. There is seldom one approach that is "the correct" approach; it is more important to consider what is the most effective way to help the students understand the concepts. This involves careful consideration of the content and the most appropriate teaching strategy. After teaching the basic concepts, you should proceed with teaching any necessary skills that students need to successfully apply the concepts during the group work activity or in the future. For example, if students are learning about comparing or contrasting animal characteristics, and will need to complete a Venn diagram during the group work, then it is important to teach them how to make and fill in a Venn diagram during the mini-lesson. Another example is if students are expected to make a rhythmic pattern, you can create one pattern as a whole group to practice this skill.

The mini-lesson is important because it not only provides the students with new knowledge, but it is also an opportunity for the teacher to assess students' understanding of the new concepts. While solicitation of students' answers is the preferred mode of transfer of knowledge, it is sometimes necessary for the teacher to provide an explanation to clarify a topic for the students. In general, the mini-lesson should take about 10-15 minutes in order to adequately address the main concepts.

In addition to listing the activities and key questions and answers, in the mini-lesson you should also include instructions about how you will utilize your materials, and this should be typed in italics. For example, you should clearly state when you will be writing definitions on the dry erase board or when you are having students come up to participate in the activity. Additionally, you should state when you will be handing out any materials to the students during this part of the lesson.

The key questions in the mini-lesson are meant to continually assess student understanding, while stimulating students' thinking abilities. Students will often convey misconceptions about the topic in their answers to the key questions; therefore, your follow-up questions are critical in helping them to construct a new understanding of the topic. If students continue to have difficulty with the answer, they may need a clear example or statement to explain the concept clearly. It is assumed that this follow-up will be part of your procedure during the lesson, and it is therefore not necessary to explicitly write this out in your lesson plan.

Example Science, Comparing Temperature, 1st Grade CTT

Mini-Lesson (15 minutes)

1. I will introduce the vocabulary terms to the students.
   I will write the definitions on the dry erase board as I discuss them with students.

    A. We will discuss the definition and application of the term temperature.
       o Can anyone tell me what the word temperature means? (the hotness or coldness of an object)
       o For what purposes have you heard the word temperature used? (the temperature outside, when I'm sick, answers will vary)

    B. We will discuss the definition and application of the term thermometer.
       o Does anyone know what instrument we use to measure the temperature? (thermometer)
       o When have you seen a thermometer before? (when I was sick, at the doctor, answers will vary)

2. I will take out a large model paper thermometer.
       o Who knows what we call this instrument? (thermometer)

3. We will discuss how to read the thermometer.
       o What do the numbers on the thermometer represent? (degrees)
       o Do the numbers at the top represent hot temperature or cold temperature? (hot)
       o How about the numbers at the bottom? (cold)
       o What do you think the red line represents? (the top of the red line tells us the temperature)

4. I will ask the students about where the red line on the thermometer will be in different seasons.
   I will have a student come up to adjust the red line on the thermometer as I ask the following questions.
   - o Where will the red line be in winter? (bottom of the thermometer near 32 degrees)
   - o Where will the red line be in summer? (top of the thermometer near 80 degrees)

5. I will ask the students about where the red line on the thermometer will be in different locations.
   I will fill out a prediction chart on the dry erase board with the student predictions as they answer the following questions.
   - o Where will the red line be in the classroom during any season? (correct answer – 70 degrees; student answers will vary)
   - o What do you think the temperature is outside right now in the sun? (answer will depend on the season and weather)
   - o What do you think the temperature is outside right now in the shade? (answer will depend on the season and weather)

☑ Exercise F

Fill in the questions and answers for the following activity statements.

♪ Music — I will discuss with students about the value of a quarter note and half note.

- _____ (Answer _____)
- _____ (Answer _____)
- _____ (Answer _____)

π Math — I will review with students the different types of polygons.

- _____ (Answer _____)
- _____ (Answer _____)
- _____ (Answer _____)

⚗ Science — I will review with students the definition of texture and luster of rocks.

- _____ (Answer _____)
- _____ (Answer _____)
- _____ (Answer _____)

✓ Exercise G

Review the following section of a mini-lesson and determine what elements are done incorrectly. Then, on a separate sheet of paper, write a correct version of each of the examples.

♪ Music

1. I will introduce various musical instruments to the students.

   I will hold up picture cards of various instruments (violin, keyboard, drum, flute) while asking the following questions.
   - o What is the name of this instrument? (Answers will vary)
   - o What is the category that each instrument belongs to? (Answers will vary)

🧪 Science

2. I will test various objects for the students to see which float and sink.
   - o I will place objects in water as students give their predictions about which will float and sink.
   - o Do you think this object will float or sink? (Students will state their prediction)
   - o I will write student predictions on the dry erase board.
   - o I will test the objects for the students to see which float and sink.

π Math

3. I will discuss the line of symmetry.
   - o I will tell students this is a line of symmetry.
   - o I will have students fold different shapes to create 2 equal parts.
   - o I will show students a picture of a butterfly and draw a line down the middle.

   Do you notice anything about the two sides of the butterfly?
   (Expected answer: They are the same.)

For Your Information

Occasionally, you may see lesson plans that have direct quotations of what the teacher will say. For example, "Today, students, we will be talking about the topic of sound waves…." We are not encouraging the use of direct quotations because it is common for new teachers to depend too much on their written lesson plan. Rather than being focused on specific dialogue, your language should be flexible in order to interact with and respond to children appropriately.

Additionally, there are different ways to write the activity statements for your lesson, including using "I will" statements from the teacher's perspective or "the children will…" from the students' perspective. In either case, it is important to be clear about who will be doing the activity. For example, if the students are sharing their results from the group work, then the activity statement should say either "I will ask the students to share their results…" or "The children will share their results with the group…" It is not correct in this case to state: "I will share the results with the children" or "The group will share the results."

Group Work

Group work is an activity that students will complete while working with at least one other student. The purpose of group work is to help students develop collaborative skills, such as sharing, communicating, problem-solving, and learning from each other. Working with a partner or group, students begin to learn their own strengths and weaknesses, and how to use their different abilities when interacting with others.

When designing an activity for group work, it is useful to consider Vygotsky's zone of proximal development. According to Vygotsky, the zone of proximal development is "the distance between the actual developmental level as determined by independent problem solving and the level of potential development as determined through problem solving under adult guidance, or in collaboration with more capable peers" (Vygotsky, 1978). In applying this to your group work, this means that your group work activity should involve a problem that is challenging for the students, but that most students will be able to accomplish with their peers with minimal assistance from the teacher.

For the group work, the teacher should begin by giving clear instructions to the students about the expectations for the group work, including the steps involved in the activity and also proper use of materials. It is important not to give out the materials while you are giving instructions because students will immediately be distracted and begin to play with the materials. In your lesson plan, you should explicitly state: a) behavioral expectations, b) proper use of the materials, and c) specific instructions for the group work. By anticipating what students may do wrong during the activity, it is often possible to prevent these unwanted actions from occurring. For example, you may write an activity statement, such as:

I will explain the following expectations to the students:
- o Share the materials with your partner(s).
- o Do not splash the water, or the water will be taken away.
- o Make sure to pass the scissors to others by covering the sharp end, and only cut the materials given to you for this activity.
- o Don't eat the materials (sugar, salt, oil, etc).
- o Do not touch the musical instruments with wet hands.

While students are working, the teacher should circulate around to the different groups to make sure that students understand the instructions and are working appropriately together. The teacher should allow the students some time to solve their own questions and negotiate the use of materials. The teacher needs to judge when it is necessary to step in and assist the students.

The teacher should have prepared questions to ask students as they are working on their project to make sure that they are understanding the concepts and making appropriate connections. A good time to ask students these questions is when they need to be refocused on the activity, or when they have completed a majority of the task. This is an opportunity for the teacher to assess the depth of students' understanding of the topic. Any confusion or misconceptions can be further addressed during the share and conclusion parts of the lesson.

When students are finished their group work, it is wise to have them clean up their space, and the teacher should put away any materials that are no longer needed. If some students finish earlier than others, the teacher should check their work to make sure the activity has been completed thoroughly (often students will not completely fill out the worksheet that goes with the activity). If the activity is complete, then the teacher may give students a challenge task as an extension to the group work. For example, if students are testing objects to see if they float or sink, and they have tested all eight objects that they were given, then the teacher may have these students choose three objects from the classroom to test. Another option is to have a back-up worksheet for students to complete when they are finished early.

For Your Information

In place of group work, it may be more appropriate in some lessons to have the students work individually to apply or practice what was taught during the mini-lesson. In this case, this section of the lesson plan is called 'Coached Practice.' During this part of the lesson, students will work independently to complete the applied task. Examples of activities during coached practice include problem solving, working on individual projects such as creating a story, applying formulas to practice problems, and so forth. Through coached practice the teacher can help individual children learn, based on his/her own developmental needs. The teacher can accomplish this by circulating throughout the classroom to work one-on-one with students.

> **Example** Science, Comparing Temperature, 1st Grade CTT

Group Work (15 minutes)

1. I will explain to students about the group work.
   A. I will explain the procedure (listed below) that the students will be doing for the group work
   B. I will explain what materials (thermometer, pencil and observation worksheet) they will be using for the group work
   C. I will discuss the expectations for proper behavior during group work:
      o Share the materials with your partner(s).
      o Take turns using the thermometer and writing your observations.
      o Be careful not to drop the thermometer, and if the thermometer breaks, do not touch it and tell the teacher immediately.
      o When going outdoors, make sure to stay with the group.
      o Stay focused on the class's activity.
2. I will divide students into groups of two and then give out the worksheet to the students, and students will write their prediction about the temperature in the three locations (inside the classroom, outside in the sun, outside in the shade).
3. After students have written their predictions, I will give students their thermometer and they will measure and record the temperature in the classroom.
4. After all groups have recorded the indoor temperature, students will line up to go outside to measure the temperature.
5. We will go as a group to measure the temperature in a sunny location and then in a shady location. Students will each use their own thermometer and record the temperature on their worksheets.
6. While students are measuring the temperature, I will walk around to see if they need any assistance, and will ask them the following questions:
   o What was the temperature in the classroom? (Should be around 70 degrees)
   o What was the temperature in the sun/shade? (Will depend on season and weather)
   o Why do you think the temperature was different inside and outside? (Inside the temperature is controlled by the heat or air conditioning, and is separated from the outside by walls; outside the temperature is determined by the season and weather)
   o Why do you think the temperature was different in the sun and in the shade? (the sun heats up the air, and this does not happen in the shade)
7. After students have completed their measurements, we will go back inside the classroom and students will return their thermometers to the correct drawer.

☑ Exercise H

List some rules for the following group work activity.

🧪 Science

1. Students are comparing the weight of various rocks using a simple balance scale.

   _____
   _____
   _____
   _____

π Math

2. Students are using pattern blocks to fill a larger shape.

   _____
   _____
   _____
   _____

♪ Music

3. Students are making a rhythmic pattern of 4 beats to a measure, using different musical notes.

   _____
   _____
   _____
   _____

Share

The ***share*** section of your lesson plan is an opportunity for students to share the results of their group work with other students in the class. Sharing the results can be done more formally by having each group come to the front of the class and present their results one group at a time. In this case, each group should present a limited number of results (one or two), perhaps the ones they found most interesting or the first one or two in the order they are listed on an observation worksheet, or to show their product, creation, and so forth. A less formal option for the share is to have students stay in their seats and take turns sharing their answers with the group. The teacher will ask each group to present and then go on to the next group. It may be useful during the share to record the various results on a class chart, so that all of the results can be compared visually. This is very helpful for visual learners.

It is important for students to have the opportunity to share their results as it builds their skills and confidence in presenting information to others. This part of the lesson is also important for the teacher to assess students' understanding of their results, and to clarify any incorrect findings or misconceptions. In order to do this, the teacher should ask each group questions during their presentation of the results. The teacher can also ask other groups whether they agree or not with the group presenting, which also functions to keep all students engaged while each group is presenting.

In your written lesson plan, you should indicate if students are coming to the front to present or staying in their seats, and what students will be presenting to others. You should also list the key questions that you will ask to the presenting groups and other groups.

Example Science, Comparing Temperature, 1st Grade CTT

Share (5 minutes)

1. I will ask the students what results they found for each of the locations (inside the classroom, outside in the sun, outside in the shade). One group will present their answer for each location, and then I will ask the other groups if they have anything different.
I will record the students' answers on a chart on the dry erase board.

2. As students are presenting, I will ask the following questions:

- o What was the temperature in the classroom? (Should be around 70 degrees)

- o Did any of the groups get a different result? (Yes/no) If yes, what was the temperature your group found? (Answers will vary)

- o What was the temperature in the sun/shade? (Will depend on season and weather)

- o Did any of the groups get a different result? (Yes/no) If yes, what was the temperature your group found? (Answers will vary)

- o Why do you think the temperature was different inside and outside? (Inside the temperature is controlled by the heat or air conditioning, and is separated from the outside by walls; outside the temperature is determined by the season and weather)

- o Why do you think the temperature was different in the sun and in the shade? (the sun heats up the air, and this does not happen in the shade)

Conclusion

The *conclusion* section of your lesson plan includes a review of the main topics of the lesson and an informal assessment of student learning. The conclusion consists of a series of questions designed to review the vocabulary from the lesson and the major concepts taught. Although these questions may be similar to ones used in the lesson, the correct answer should still be included in parentheses. Some final thinking questions should also be included to extend students' comprehension and help them to make connections and transfer their knowledge. While thinking questions are essential, make sure that these questions do not involve teaching an entirely new topic to the students.

Example Science, Comparing Temperature, 1st Grade CTT

Conclusion (5 minutes)

1. I will review the main vocabulary from the lesson with the students.
    - What did we learn about today? (temperature)
    - What is the definition of temperature? (the hotness or coldness of an object)
    - How did we measure the temperature? (using a thermometer)

2. I will ask the students the following questions about the activity:
    - In what locations did we measure the temperature today? (in the classroom, outside in the sun, outside in the shade)
    - How was the temperature different in the various locations? (answers will vary depending on the season and weather)
    - Why was the temperature different in the different locations? (Inside the temperature is controlled by the heat or air conditioning, and is separated from the outside by walls; outside the sun heats up the air, and this does not happen in the shade)

3. I will ask the following questions to encourage students' thinking:
    - What do you think will be the temperature in the classroom tomorrow? (about 70 degrees or room temperature) Why? (because the conditions will be the same in the classroom)
    - What do you think will be the temperature outside tomorrow? Why? (answers will vary depending on the season and weather)
    - Where could we look to find out the prediction for the outside temperature tomorrow? (newspaper, internet, tv, answers will vary)

Time Allotment

The time for each section should be included in parentheses next to the title of the section. It is important to include the time for each section so that your lesson flows well and there is enough time to complete each section. Writing the time also ensures that you will think through the proportion of time that should be spent on each section. This will make it easier during the lesson if the total lesson time is either shortened or lengthened. It is also common that a section of the lesson plan will take longer or shorter to complete when actually teaching it; this means that you will have to adjust the times for the remaining sections proportionately so that you have time to complete the whole lesson.

> **For Your Information**
>
> If you are the primary classroom teacher, then you will have the opportunity to continue a lesson either later in the day or the next day. This may be beneficial if students need more time to complete part of the lesson. As the classroom teacher, you will need to balance the time spent on each topic in your curriculum with the students' learning needs.

For a 45 minute lesson, a recommended time allotment is:

Introduction	(3-5 minutes)
Motivation	(5-7 minutes)
Mini-Lesson	(10-15 minutes)
Group Work	(15 minutes)
Share	(5 minutes)
Conclusion	(5 minutes)

Formative Assessment

Assessment refers to the process of measuring learning outcomes in an educational context. Within a lesson, teachers use both **formal** and **informal assessments** to measure student achievement and comprehension. The main difference between these forms of assessment is that formal assessments are graded, while informal assessments are not graded. Examples of formal assessments include: quizzes, tests, worksheets, lab reports, graded projects, essays, etc. Examples of informal assessments include: observations, questioning, interviewing, conversation, etc. (see *Figure 2* below)

All of the formal and informal assessments included in a lesson are referred to as **formative assessments.** In your lesson plan, this will include a list of the different informal and formal methods of assessment that you are using during your lesson to measure student understanding. It is important that these assessment methods are aligned with the objectives for the lesson, so that all cognitive, affective, and psychomotor objectives are assessed during the lesson, as can be seen in each of the lessons in *Figure 1* below.

Figure 1. **Three Lesson Unit** *(based on Standards for Unit)*

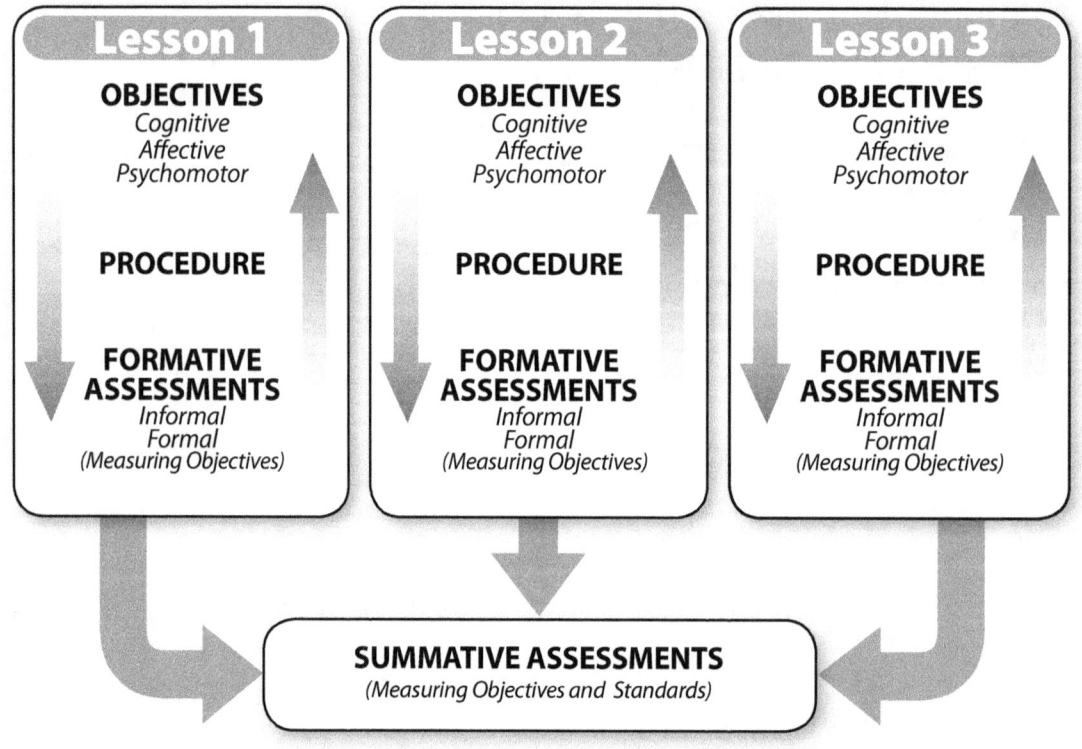

When writing a series of lesson plans for a unit, then it is common to end the unit with a *summative assessment* that will measure student learning for the whole unit. A summative assessment is most commonly in the form of a quiz or exam, but may also include a performance-based assessment, such as a project or presentation. Examples of the various types of assessment and their relationships are provided in *Figure 2*.

Figure 2. **Types of Assessment**

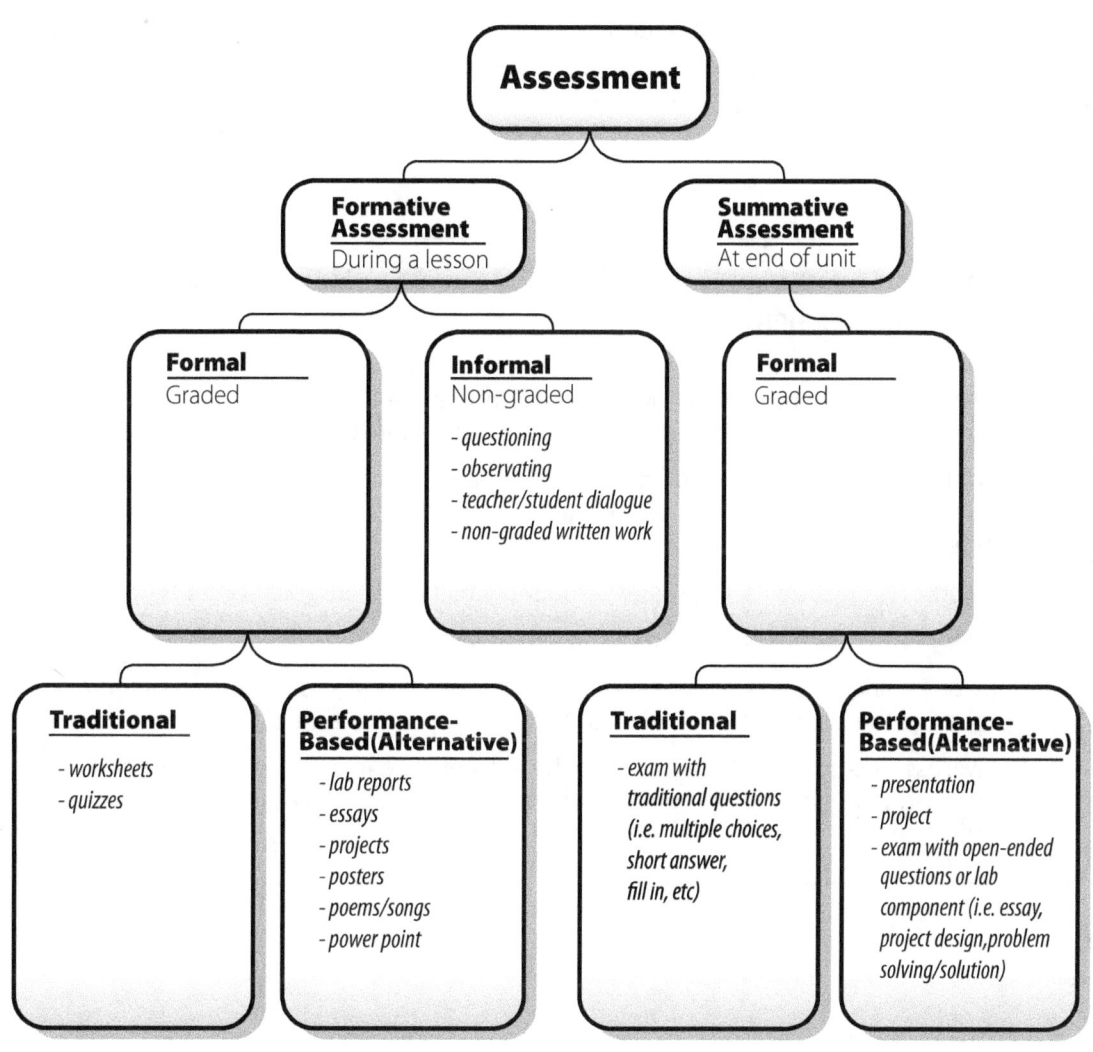

LESSON PLAN CONTENTS

> **For Your Information**
>
> When using a **performance-based (alternative) assessment**, it is necessary to create a grading rubric to measure student achievement. A rubric is a tool designed for an activity or project to aid in assessment of student performance in a variety of categories. Ideally, this rubric will be shared with the students when they are given instructions for completing the assessment. Some teachers will even have students participate in creation of the rubric in order to create a more communal learning environment (Bagley, 2010). Another advantage of performance-based assessment is that it is possible to differentiate the assignment for different types of learners. For example, students may have an option to complete a summative assessment project in the form of a written paper, poster, or presentaion.

Example — Science, Comparing Temperature, 1st Grade CTT

Formative Assessment

1. I will assess students' prior knowledge of temperature and using a thermometer through questioning during the introduction and motivation (cognitive objective).

2. I will assess student understanding of temperatures in different locations through questioning during the mini-lesson, group work, share, and conclusion (cognitive objective).

3. By observing students, I will assess students' ability to work collaboratively with their partner during group work (affective objective).

4. By observing students, I will assess their ability to properly use a thermometer to measure the temperature in various locations (psychomotor objective).

5. I will assess students' ability to record the temperature in degrees Fahrenheit by reviewing the observations on their organizational worksheet (psychomotor objective).

☑ Exercise I

State both a formal and informal method to assess students' achievement of the following objectives:

♪ Music — Beat and Rhythm, 2nd Grade

1. Upon completion of the lesson, students will….
   - Identify the name and values of musical symbols, such as whole note, half note, quarter note, and eighth note.

Informal Assessment: _____

Formal Assessment: _____

♪ Music — Beat and Rhythm, 2nd Grade

2. Upon completion of the lesson, students will….
   - Create a rhythmic pattern of 3 or 4 beats using different musical notes

Informal Assessment: _____

Formal Assessment: _____

π Math — Telling Time on Analog Clocks, 2nd Grade

3. Upon completion of the lesson, students will….
   - Correctly display time to five minute intervals on an analog clock.

Informal Assessment: _____

Formal Assessment: _____

Handouts

The ***handouts*** for your lesson are written or visual materials that you are giving out to the students during the lesson. The handouts may include a vocabulary list, worksheet, picture cards, visual representation, poem, lyrics of a song, and so forth. Each of the handouts needs to be listed in the materials section, included with the lesson plan, and clearly labeled as to in which section it will be utilized. You may adapt handouts from existing sources, but it is required that you always list the source and highly recommended that you modify the handout to fit with your lesson appropriately. Graphic organizers are very useful for young children to help them record their ideas or results while they are completing an activity. Remember, it can take young children a while to write out their ideas, so in some cases it is a good idea to provide choices that students can circle. Also, make sure to include enough space for students to write, as young children require more space than older children or adults.

Extension/Follow-up Activity

The extension activity is an additional activity that students can do if there is extra time at the end of the lesson. This activity should not be more than 5 minutes, should be directly related to the content of the lesson, and age-appropriate. Appropriate extension activities may include worksheets, drawings with labels, writing about the topic/lesson, and so forth. Inappropriate activities include: coloring-only activities, word searches, and so forth. Make sure that the extension activity does not involve teaching an entirely new topic to the students. The extension activity may also be used as an opportunity to challenge those students who were excelling during the lesson, and also to provide extra help for students who are struggling with the topic.

Example 1 — Music, Beat and Rhythm, 2nd Grade

Create 5 more rhythmic patterns in a measure on your worksheet.

Example 2 — Science, Comparing Temperature, 1st Grade CTT

Draw a picture of the places where you measured the temperature today and label them with the correct temperature.

Example 3 — Math, Telling Time on Analog Clocks, 2nd grade

For each activity listed on the worksheet (eating breakfast, going to school, etc.) use the clock next to the activity to display the time you do that activity during your day.

REFERENCES

Bagley, S.S. (2010). Students, teachers and alternative assessment in secondary school: Relational Models Theory (RMT) in the field of education. *The Australian Educational Researcher*, 37(1), 83-106.

Vygotsky, L. (1978). Mind in Society, Cambridge, MA: Harvard University Press

Websites

Science Standards

NYC K-8 Science Scope and Sequence
http://schools.nyc.gov/Documents/STEM/Science/K8ScienceSS.pdf

National Science Education Standards (1996). National Research Council. Washington, DC: National Academy Press.
http://www.nap.edu/html/nses/

New York State Learning Standards and Core Curriculum
http://www.p12.nysed.gov/ciai/cores.html

New York State Science Core Curricula for Regents Courses
http://schools.nyc.gov/Academics/Science/EducatorResources/New+York+State+Science+Core+Curricula.htm

NYC High School Science Regents Scope & Sequence
http://schools.nyc.gov/Documents/STEM/Science/HSScienceSSRegents.pdf

Math Standards

New York State Core Curriculum (revised 2005)
http://www.p12.nysed.gov/ciai/mst/math/standards/core.html

Common Core State Standards Initiative
http://www.corestandards.org/about-the-standards

Music Standards

State Standards for Arts developed by New York State School Music Association (NYSSMA)
http://www.p12.nysed.gov/ciai/arts/pub/artlearn.pdf

National Music Education Standards by National Association for Music Education (MENC)
http://www.menc.org/resources/view/the-school-music-program-a-new-vision

GLOSSARY OF TERMS

Affective Objectives: Educational outcomes targeting the awareness and growth in attitudes, emotion, and feelings

Alternative Assessment: See performance-based assessment

Assessment: The process of measuring learning outcomes in an educational context

Beat: Steady pulse of the sound

Behavioral Objectives: See psychomotor objectives

Cognitive Objectives: Educational outcomes revolving around knowledge and comprehension

Dry-erase Board: A board with a glossy white surface for nonpermanent markings; also known as a whiteboard

Eighth note: A musical symbol, in common time, having the value of 1/2 beat

Extension (Follow-up) activity: Additional activity students can do if extra time at the end of the lesson

Formal Assessment: Structured and measured assessment

Formative Assessment: Assessment to measure students' understanding within a lesson

Group Work: A form of collaborative learning with two or more people

Half note: A musical symbol, in common time, having the value of two beats

Handouts: Written or visual materials given out to students

Informal Assessment: Assessment that is not graded and usually done by observation or dialogue

Measure: Visual representation of meter

Meter: Grouping of beats

Mini-lesson: A section of the lesson to teach the key concepts

Motivation: An activity of the lesson to get students engaged

Objectives: Measurable or observable outcomes

Performance-based assessment: A non-traditional type of assessment such as a project or presentation that evaluates the students on what they know or can do from their demonstration or the creation of a product

Pitch: Highness or lowness of sound

Psychomotor Objectives: Learning outcomes for the development of physical skills and often involving manipulation of materials

Quarter note: A musical symbol, in common time, having the value of one beat

Rhythm: Combination of long and short sounds

Summative Assessment: Assessment of learning that summarizes the development of learners for a unit of study

Temperature: The degree or intensity of heat present in a substance or object

Tempo: Fastness or slowness of music

Thermometer: An instrument for measuring the temperature of a substance or object

Whole note: A musical symbol, in common time, having the value of four beats

Worksheet: A handout developed to either convey concepts to students, provide an organizational system aiding students in recording information, or asking questions to be answered in written form by the students

Zone of Proximal Development: The distance between the actual developmental level as determined by independent problem solving and the level of potential development as determined through problem solving under adult guidance, or in collaboration with more capable peers

APPENDIX A

Lesson Plan Comments

Pre-requisite Knowledge

PK1: Remember – prerequisite knowledge is what they need to know before the lesson. What you have listed is part of what you are going to teach them, so it shouldn't be listed as pre-requisite knowledge.

PK2: Pre-requisite knowledge should not include experiences outside of school that are not necessary for the lesson.

PK3: Your lesson assumes they have other prior knowledge in addition to that which you have listed.

Vocabulary

V1: These terms are too advanced for XX grade.

V2: You need to add dictionary and kid-friendly definitions for the terms.

V3: You have included kid-friendly definitions, but you need to add dictionary definitions for the terms as well.

V4: You have included dictionary definitions, but you need to add kid-friendly definitions for the terms as well.

V5: Your dictionary definition includes too much technical jargon. Find one that is easier to understand.

V6: Your kid-friendly definition does not convey the same meaning as the dictionary meaning. It needs to convey the same meaning in simpler terms.

V7: Your kid-friendly definition is not age-appropriate. It needs to be in simple language the children can understand.

Standards

S1: You also need to list the process and inquiry standards your lesson addresses from the first two pages of the NYC K-8 Scope and Sequence.

S2: You only have process and inquiry standards listed – you need to add your content standard here as well.

S3: The standards need to be divided and labeled as process, inquiry, and content standards.

S4: You only have content standards listed – you need process standards here as well.

S5: You only have content standard listed – you need to add your achievement standard here as well.

S6: Standard you listed is not matching what you are teaching in your lesson.

S7: You should include all applicable standards.

Objectives

General Comments:

OG1: Your objectives do not match with your lesson contents and/or activities.

OG2: You should include all objectives you cover in your lesson.

OG3: Your objectives are not appropriate for the age level you are teaching.

Cognitive:

OC1: You need to be more specific about the elements you want them to know. Specific examples should either be written out or listed in parentheses.

OC2: This is a psychomotor objective because it involves a physical skill. A cognitive objective involves a thinking task.

Affective:

OA1: This is a cognitive objective which involves a thinking task. Affective objectives should be attitude/dispositional achievements that include communication, sharing, working in groups, etc.

OA2: This is a psychomotor objective because it involves a physical skill. Affective objectives include communication, sharing, working in groups, etc.

OA3: Sharing (= presenting) is different from sharing with others.

Psychomotor:

OP1: Your psychomotor objectives should indicate the physical action/skills students will be performing.

OP2: Only this objective is psychomotor – it must involve physical action.

OP3: You should also add an objective about recording their results on a worksheet.

OP4: This is what the students will do in an activity. Psychomotor objective should include what they will achieve through the activity.

OP5: This objective involves a thinking task, and therefore is a cognitive objective rather than a psychomotor objective.

Materials

M1: You need to state how many students you are providing materials for and how many groups you will have.

M2: You need to list how many of each item.

M3: You need to list how many of these you are giving each group.

M4: Your materials list should be in a list format with bullet points.

M5: You should write the name and author of the book/poem here.

M6: You are missing items from your materials list.

M7: You need to include the worksheets in your materials list.

M8: You should add the visual aids you are using in your mini-lesson.

All Procedure Sections

PS1: You need to rewrite this section in outline format, with each of the activities clearly numbered, and the key questions/answers bulleted under each activity.

PS2: You need an activity statement describing your intention with these questions.

PS3: What are your key questions/answers here? Add them here as a bullet point list.

PS4: These questions should be listed with bullet points below the activity.

PS5: Your question is not appropriate for the activity statement.

PS6: Your question is too vague for the children to answer.

PS7: Your question and/or answers should be written in a kid-friendly manner.

PS8: This is an inaccurate term (or explanation) in this context.

PS9: Rather than "explaining" to students, you should list the specific questions you will ask students to guide the discussion.

PS10: You do not need to write directly what you will say to the students. You should replace this with an activity statement instead.

PS11: This part/questions are not appropriate for this section.

Introduction

I1: You need an intro statement about the activity. For example, "I will begin the lesson by asking students the following questions:…"

I2: What are some expected answers to this question? Add in parentheses after writing "Expected answers:…."

I3: This question is not relevant to your lesson content. You should replace it with a more relevant question.

I4: You should begin with a more open-ended question here.

I5: You should not list questions which are not related to each other.

I6: Your questions do not flow from one to another.

I7: You have listed many questions, but they are unrelated to each other. What is your goal for this section?

Motivation

M1: You should list some key questions/answers you will ask the students either during or after reading the book/poem.

M2: You should add some other key questions/answers about the book/poem.

M3: What is/are the correct answer(s) to this question? Add in parentheses after question.

M4: This is redundant with what you are asking in the introduction.

Mini-Lesson

ML1: You need a statement here of the activity, such as: "I will begin the mini-lesson by asking students:.."

ML2: Your mini-lesson needs to be reformatted into outline form by numbering your activity statements with each set of questions bulleted underneath. I started the formatting for you, but you need to finish it.

ML3: You need to introduce the vocabulary words ___ and ___ here.

ML4: Students will not be familiar with this term, so you need to explain it before asking about it.

ML5: You do not need to teach this concept or term here.

ML6: You need to describe how you will be using (or handing out) the materials here with an instruction statement.

ML7: You should use a dry erase board for this part of the lesson. This needs to be indicated here and in your materials list.

ML8: What is/are the correct answer(s) to this question? Add in parentheses after question.

ML9: This is not the correct answer to this question.

ML10: This should be part of the group work section below.

ML11: Your mini-lesson is not substantial enough (too simple and short) to teach the concepts.

ML12: Your lesson needs to be re-organized in proper order (what should come first and next, etc.); it is difficult to follow.

ML13: Try to ask this in a way that provokes students' thinking.

ML14: Your mini-lesson focuses too much on transmitting knowledge and not enough on the other domains.

ML15 (music-specific): You should perform or ask the students to perform while explaining these terms.

ML16: You need to do more examples with the students before proceeding to the next step.

Group Work

G1: You need to divide them into groups first, and list how many students per group. This should be indicated here.

G2: You need to add here that you are handing out the materials and what the materials are.

G3: Are the students filling out a worksheet together or individually? This should be indicated here.

G4: What are your instructions to the students? These should be listed here.

G5: You should give clear instructions about the correct way to use the ___ here.

G6: What key questions/answers will you ask students as they are performing their group work? These should be listed here.

G7: What is/are the correct answer(s) to this question? Add in parentheses after question.

G8: Your question here is not appropriate.

G9: This is not the correct answer to this question.

G10: You must not only explain the activity, but demonstrate what you expect them to do.

Share

SH1: You need to add an instruction statement in italics about how you will have students present (come up to the front, stay in the seats, etc).

SH2: You should have each group present just one or two results because all the items will take too long. This should be specified here.

SH3: What key questions/answers will you ask students as they are presenting their group work? These should be listed here.

SH4: What is/are the correct answer(s) to this question? Add in parentheses after question.

Conclusion

C1: You need an intro activity statement here, such as: "I will review the lesson with students through the following questions:…"

C2: You should add review questions/answers to assess if students learned the vocabulary.

C3: You should add review questions/answers to assess what students learned from the group work activity.

C4: You should add some thinking questions to challenge students, applying what they've learned to a new context or set of examples.

C5: You should review what was covered in your lesson. You cannot teach new concepts in conclusion.

C6: Your review should be a summary of the contents. You should not repeat the whole procedure.

Time Allotment

T1: You need to write the time for this section here.

T2: You have too much time allotted for this section.

T3: You have too little time allotted for this section.

Formative Assessment

FA1: You need to state how you will assess the cognitive, affective, and psychomotor objectives during the different parts of the lesson. The type of objective should be listed in parentheses.

FA2: You are missing an assessment of your cognitive objectives. This needs to be added.

FA3: You are missing an assessment of your affective objectives.

FA4: You are missing an assessment of your psychomotor objectives. This needs to be added.

FA5: You should add that you will be assessing them throughout the lesson through questioning and listening to their answers (cognitive).

Handouts

H1: You need to include all of your handouts with your lesson plan.

H2: Your handouts need to be labeled so that it is clear which section of the procedure it will be used in.

H3: This handout is not age-appropriate as it is for a more advanced level.

H4: The spaces for writing on your handout are too small for young children. You should provide larger spaces for them to write.

Extension

E1: This is a good extension activity – you need to include the handout with your lesson plan.

E2: This extension activity is a bit too complicated, as it should only require about 5 minutes. You should think of a simpler activity.

E3: This extension activity involves teaching a totally new topic. You should think of a different activity that reinforces what you have done during the lesson.

E4: This extension activity is redundant because it was already done in your procedure. Think of a different activity that reinforces the same concept in different ways.

APPENDIX B

Example of Science Lesson Plan

LESSON INFORMATION
Subject: Science
Topic: Comparing Temperatures
Lesson Number: 2
Teaching Date: April 9, 2012
Grade Level: 1st Grade CTT

PREREQUISITE KNOWLEDGE
Students should be familiar with concepts related to hot and cold, and students should know the difference between inside and outside.

VOCABULARY
1. Temperature: the degree or intensity of heat present in a substance or object
   [Kid-friendly] *the amount of heat in an object*
2. Thermometer: an instrument for measuring the temperature of a substance or object
   [Kid-friendly] *a tool used for measuring how hot or cold something is*

NYC K-8 Science Standards

Content Standard:
PS 1.1a, PS 3.1g Compare temperatures in different locations (e.g., inside, outside, in the sun, in the shade).

Inquiry Skills:
Gathering and organizing data – *collecting information about objects and events which illustrate a specific situation*
Manipulating materials – *handling or treating materials and equipment safely, skillfully, and effectively*

Process Skills:
iv. Manipulate materials through teacher direction and free discovery.
xx. Compare and contrast organisms/objects/events in the living and physical environments.

OBJECTIVES

Cognitive Objectives
By the end of the lesson, students will be able to:
- Compare temperatures in different locations, including inside and outside the classroom, in the sun, and in the shade.

Affective Objectives
By the end of the lesson, students will be able to:
- Work collaboratively with their partner during group work
- Share their results with their classmates during the "share" activity

Psychomotor Objectives
By the end of the lesson, students will be able to:
- Use a thermometer to measure temperature in different locations, including inside and outside the classroom, in the sun, and in the shade.
- Record the temperature in degrees Fahrenheit in an organizational chart

MATERIALS *(12 students, 6 groups)*
- 2 Beakers
- Sink to fill up beakers
- 7 Thermometers (1 for motivation, 1 per group)
- 1 Dry Erase Board
- 2 Dry Erase Markers
- 1 Large Model Thermometer
- 6 Worksheets for Group Work (1 per group)
- 6 Pencils for Group Work (1 per group)
- 12 Pieces of Construction Paper
- 4 Boxes of Crayons/Markers

PROCEDURE

Introduction (3 minutes)
I will begin the lesson by asking students the following questions:
- o Can anyone tell me what the temperature is like outside today?

(Expected Answer: hot cold, answers may vary depending on season)
- Does anyone know the name of the instrument we use to measure the temperature? (Expected Answer: thermometer)
- Can anyone tell me where they have seen a thermometer before? (Expected Answer: when I was sick, at the doctor's office, answers may vary)

Motivation (5 minutes)
1. I will fill up two beakers with water of two different temperatures (cold and warm).
2. I will pass around the beakers and have students feel the different temperatures of the water with a finger.
3. I will ask students:
   - How do you think we could find out the temperature of the water in each beaker? (Expected Answer: use a thermometer)
4. I will take out a thermometer and place it in the beaker with cold water.
5. I will have a student close to me read the temperature on the thermometer in Fahrenheit.
   - What is the temperature of the cold water? (Expected Answer: around 50 degrees F)
6. I will ask the students:
   - What do you think will be the temperature of the warm water? (Expected Answer: answers will vary)
7. I will then move the thermometer to the beaker with warm water.
8. I will have a student close to me read the temperature on the thermometer in Fahrenheit.
   - What is the temperature of the warm water? (Expected Answer: around 80 degrees F)

Mini-Lesson (10 minutes)
1. I will introduce the vocabulary terms to the students.
   I will write the definitions on the dry erase board as I discuss them with students.
   A. We will discuss the definition and application of the term temperature.
      - Can anyone tell me what the word temperature means? (the hotness or coldness of an object)
      - For what purposes have you heard the word temperature used? (the temperature outside, when I'm sick, answers will vary)
   B. We will discuss the definition and application of the term thermometer.
      - What is the name of the instrument we just used to measure the temperature? (thermometer)
      - How could we write the definition of the word "thermometer"? (a tool for measuring how hot or cold something is)
2. I will take out a large model paper thermometer.
   - Who knows what we call this instrument? (thermometer)
3. We will discuss how to read the thermometer.

- o What do the numbers on the thermometer represent? (degrees)
- o Do the numbers at the top represent hot temperature or cold temperature? (hot)
- o How about the numbers at the bottom?(cold)
- o What do you think the red line represents? (the top of the red line tells us the temperature)

4. I will ask the students about where the red line on the thermometer will be in different seasons.
   I will have a student come up to adjust the red line on the thermometer as I ask the following questions.
   - o Where will the red line be in winter? (bottom of the thermometer near 32 degrees)
   - o Where will the red line be in summer? (top of the thermometer near 80 degrees)
5. I will ask the students about where the red line on the thermometer will be in different locations.
   I will fill out a prediction chart on the dry erase board with the student predictions as they answer the following questions.
   - o Where will the red line be in the classroom during any season? (correct answer – 70 degrees; student answers will vary)
   - o What do you think the temperature is outside right now in the sun? (answer will depend on the season and weather)
   - o What do you think the temperature is outside right now in the shade? (answer will depend on the season and weather)

Group Work (15 minutes)

1. I will introduce the group work activity to the students.
   A. I will explain the procedure (listed below) that the students will be doing for the group work
   B. I will explain what materials (thermometer, pencil and observation worksheet) they will be using for the group work
   C. I will discuss the expectations for proper behavior during group work:
      - o Share the materials with your partner(s).
      - o Take turns using the thermometer and writing your observations.
      - o Be careful not to drop the thermometer, and if the thermometer breaks, do not touch it and tell the teacher immediately.
      - o When going outdoors, make sure to stay with the group.
      - o Stay focused on the class's activity.
2. I will divide the students into groups of 2, and give out one worksheet to each pair of students.
3. Students will write their prediction about the temperature in the three locations (inside the classroom, outside in the sun, outside in the shade).
4. After students have written their predictions, I will give students their thermometer and they will measure and record the temperature in the classroom.
5. After all groups have recorded the indoor temperature, students will line up to go

outside to measure the temperature.
6. We will go as a group to measure the temperature in a sunny location and then in a shady location. Students will each use their own thermometer and record the temperature on their worksheets.
7. While students are measuring the temperature, I will walk around to see if they need any assistance, and will ask them the following questions:
    - o   What was the temperature in the classroom? (Should be around 70 degrees)
    - o   What was the temperature in the sun/shade? (Will depend on season and weather)
    - o   Why do you think the temperature was different inside and outside? (Inside the temperature is controlled by the heat or air conditioning, and is separated from the outside by walls; outside the temperature is determined by the season and weather)
    - o   Why do you think the temperature was different in the sun and in the shade? (the sun heats up the air, and this does not happen in the shade)
8. After students have completed their measurements, we will go back inside the classroom and students will return their thermometers to the correct drawer.

Share (5 minutes)
I will ask the students what results they found for each of the locations (inside the classroom, outside in the sun, outside in the shade). One group will present their answer for each location, and then I will ask the other groups if they have anything different.
I will record the students' answers on a chart on the dry erase board.
    - o   What was the temperature in the classroom? (Should be around 70 degrees)
    - o   Did any of the groups get a different result? (Yes/no) If yes, what was the temperature your group found? (Answers will vary)
    - o   What was the temperature in the sun/shade? (Will depend on season and weather)
    - o   Did any of the groups get a different result? (Yes/no) If yes, what was the temperature your group found? (Answers will vary)
    - o   Why do you think the temperature was different inside and outside? (Inside the temperature is controlled by the heat or air conditioning, and is separated from the outside by walls; outside the temperature is determined by the season and weather)
    - o   Why do you think the temperature was different in the sun and in the shade? (the sun heats up the air, and this does not happen in the shade)

Conclusion (5 minutes)
1. I will review the main vocabulary from the lesson with the students.
    - o   What did we learn about today? (temperature)
    - o   What is the definition of temperature? (the hotness or coldness of an object)
    - o   How did we measure the temperature? (using a thermometer)
2. I will ask the students the following questions about the activity:
    - o   In what locations did we measure the temperature today? (in the classroom, outside in the sun, outside in the shade)

- o How was the temperature different in the various locations? (answers will vary depending on the season and weather)
- o Why was the temperature different in the different locations? (Inside the temperature is controlled by the heat or air conditioning, and is separated from the outside by walls; outside the sun heats up the air, and this does not happen in the shade)
3. I will ask the following questions to encourage students' thinking:
    - o What do you think will be the temperature in the classroom tomorrow? (about 70 degrees or room temperature) Why? (because the conditions will be the same in the classroom)
    - o What do you think will be the temperature outside tomorrow? Why? (answers will vary depending on the season and weather)
    - o Where could we look to find out the prediction for the outside temperature tomorrow? (newspaper, internet, tv, answers will vary)

FORMATIVE ASSESSMENT

1. I will assess students' prior knowledge of temperature and using a thermometer through questioning during the introduction and motivation (cognitive objective).
2. I will assess student understanding of temperatures in different locations through questioning during the mini-lesson, group work, share, and conclusion (cognitive objective).
3. By observing students, I will assess students' ability to work collaboratively with their partner during group work (affective objective).
4. During the share, I will assess students' ability to share the results of the activity with their classmates (affective objective)
5. By observing students, I will assess their ability to properly use a thermometer to measure the temperature in various locations (psychomotor objective).
6. I will assess students' ability to record the temperature in degrees Fahrenheit by reviewing the observations on their organizational worksheet (psychomotor objective).

HANDOUTS
See handout for group work below, labeled "Group Work Handout"

EXTENSION ACTIVITY
Draw a picture of the places where you measured the temperature today and label them with the correct temperature.

GROUP WORK HANDOUT

Names of Group Members: _____

Measuring Temperature

Location	Predict	Measure
In the Classroom		
Outside in the shade		
Outside in the sun		

APPENDIX C

 Example of Music Lesson Plan

LESSON INFORMATION
Subject: Music
Topic: Beats and Rhythm
Lesson Number: 1
Teaching Date: November 24, 2012
Grade Level: 2nd Grade

PREREQUISITE KNOWLEDGE
- Students should be able to differentiate steady and non-steady sound
- Students should be able to understand whole, half, quarter, and eighth.
- *(Write more…)*

VOCABULARY
1. Beat: A metrical or rhythmic stress in music;
   [Kid-friendly] **The steady pulse of sound in music**
2. Meter: The basic recurrent rhythmical pattern of note values, accents, and beats per measure in music;
   [Kid-friendly] **Grouping of the beats**
3. *(Write more…)*

NATIONAL STANDARDS
1. Content Standard: Singing, alone and with others, a varied repertoire of music.
   Achievement Standard:
   a. Students sing, independently, in rhythm, and maintain a steady tempo
2. *(Write more…)*

OBJECTIVES

Cognitive Objectives:
Upon completion of the lesson, students will be able to…
- Define what are beat and rhythm
- Identify the proper names of the notes (whole, half, quarter, eighth note(s)) and their values.
- *(Write more…)*

Affective Objectives:
During the lesson, students will be able to…
- Work collaboratively with their partner during group work
- *(Write more…)*

Psychomotor Objectives:
By the end of the lesson, students will be able to…
- Keep the steady beat while tapping or clapping.
- *(Write more…)*

MATERIALS *(8 students, 4 groups)*
- CD player and CD 'A Singing Letter' by J. Kim for track 09. 'Click-a-click-a-click Clack'
- Visual representation set (Fruit platter model, a big size for the teacher and 8 small sets for the students): A measure (a plate), a whole note (banana), 2 half notes (apple), 4 quarter notes (kiwi), 8 eighth notes (cherry)
- *(Write more…)*

PROCEDURE
Introduction (2 mintues)
1. I will begin the lesson by asking students the following questions:
    - Does anyone know what is beat? (Expected Answer: Yes/No)
    - Can you tell me what is it? (Answers can vary)
    - *(Write more…)*

Motivation (5 minutes)
1. I will play *"Click-a-click-a-click Clack"* by Kim on the CD player and have students clap or tap to the song.
    - How did we clap/tap? (Expected answer: steady, etc.)
    - *(Write more…)*

Mini-Lesson (15 minutes)
1. I will introduce the beat concept to the students
    A. I will ask the following question:
        - We clapped steady sound to the song. Does anyone know what we call for the steady sound in music? (Beat)
    B. I will show the fish tank of my visual representation in which 4 rocks are located in the bottom evenly.
        - How many rocks to you see? (4)
        - Is it evenly located? Then, can we clap counting each rock? (one, two, three, four)
2. I will introduce different musical notes using visual representation to explain about long and short sounds.
   (Write more…)
3. I will explain how we can make rhythmic pattern with combination of long and short sounds.
   (Write more…)

Group Work (15 minutes)
1. I will explain to students about the group work.
   A. I will explain the procedure (listed below) that the students will be doing for the group work.
   B. I will explain about visual materials they will be using for the group work
      (Write more…)
   C. I will discuss the expectations for proper behavior during group work:
      - Share the materials with your partner
      - *(Write more…)*
2. I will give out the visual materials to the students, and students will make rhythmic pattern in a group of two
   (Write more…)

Share (5 minutes)
1. I will ask each group of the students come to the front and present the rhythmic pattern they made.
2. While the students present, I will ask the following questions the presenting group and/or other students:
   - What kind notes did you use to make the rhythmic pattern? (answer may vary)
   - *(Write more…)*

Conclusion (3 minutes)
1. I will review the main vocabulary from the lesson with the students.
   - What did you learn about today?
   - *(Write more…)*
2. I will ask the students the following questions about the activity:
   - What did we create in a group?
   - *(Write more…)*
3. I will ask the following questions to encourage students' thinking:
   - What are different ways to make a rhythmic pattern of four beats?
   - *(Write more…)*

ASSESSMENTS
1. I will assess students' prior knowledge of sound through questioning during the instruction (cognitive objective)
2. *(Write more…)*

EXTENSION ACTIVITY
Students will draw 5 more rhythmic patterns in a measure on a worksheet.

ABOUT THE AUTHORS

JINYOUNG KIM *is an associate professor of education at the College of Staten Island, City University of New York. She earned her Master's degree and a Doctorate in Curriculum and Instruction from Teachers College, Columbia University, specializing in early childhood education and music education. She has taught 'Music in Elementary Education' and 'Music in Early Childhood' courses for 12 years. She is the author of the books including Musical Teacher: Preparing Teachers to Use Music in the Childhood Classroom. Her research interest includes 'pre-service teachers' confidence in integrating music' and her articles have appeared in educational journals such as Journal of Research in Childhood Education. She is also a composer of children's songs and has published five music albums including 'A Singing Letter: Jinyoung Kim's Original Songs for Children.'*

ERICA BLATT *is an assistant professor of science education at the College of Staten Island, City University of New York, currently teaching courses in science teaching methods at the elementary and secondary level. Dr. Blatt earned her Ph.D. in Education from the University of New Hampshire, specializing in science education and curriculum development. At the University of New Hampshire, she taught the Practicum Seminar for the Masters of Environmental Education program for four years, while pursuing her research interests in Environmental Science education at the secondary level. Previously, she received her M.S.Ed. from the University of Pennsylvania, and taught high school Biology, Earth Science, and Environmental Science in settings as diverse as inner city Philadelphia, Phillips Academy in Andover, MA, and in Costa Rica. Dr. Blatt's research is focused upon developing environmental education curricula for the primary and secondary levels and helping teachers effectively incorporate environmental topics into their science teaching.*

www.ingramcontent.com/pod-product-compliance
Lightning Source LLC
Chambersburg PA
CBHW060518300426
44112CB00017B/2721